A Note to Parents and

Dorling Kindersley Readers is a compelling reading programme for beginning readers, designed in conjunction with leading literacy experts, including Cliff Moon, M.Ed., Honorary Fellow of the University of Reading. Cliff Moon has spent many years as a teacher and teacher educator specialising in reading and has written more than 140 books for children and teachers. He reviews regularly for teachers' journals.

Beautiful illustrations and superb full-colour photographs combine with engaging, easy-to-read stories to offer a fresh approach to each subject in the series. Each DK READER is guaranteed to capture a child's interest while developing his or her reading skills, general knowledge and love of reading.

The five levels of DK READERS are aimed at different reading abilities, enabling you to choose the books that are exactly right for your child:

Pre-level 1 – Learning to read

Level 1 – Beginning to read

Level 2 – Beginning to read alone

Level 3 – Reading alone

Level 4 – Proficient readers

The "normal" age at which a child begins to read can be anywhere from three to eight years old, so these levels are intended only as a general guideline.

No matter which level you select, you can be sure that you are helping your child learn to read, then read to learn!

LONDON, NEW YORK, MUNICH,
MELBOURNE AND DELHI

For Dorling Kindersley
Editor Kate Simkins
Designer Jon Hall
Design Manager Rob Perry
Publishing Manager Simon Beecroft
Category Publisher Alex Allan
DTP Designer Lauren Egan
Production Rochelle Talary

For Marvel
Editors Mickey Stern and Carl Suecoff

Reading Consultant
Cliff Moon, M.Ed.

This edition published in 2014
First published in Great Britain in 2006 by
Dorling Kindersley Limited,
80 Strand, London WC2R 0RL
A Penguin Random House Company

10 9 8 7 6 5 4 3 2
002-277244-Sept/14

A CIP catalogue record for this book is available from
the British Library.

ISBN 978-1-4053-1431-2

Colour reproduction by Media Development and Printing, UK
Printed and bound in China

marvel.com
© 2014 MARVEL

Discover more at
www.dk.com

Contents

THE MARVEL X-MEN SCHOOL

Written by Michael Teitelbaum

Who are the X-Men?

The X-Men are mutants. What is
a mutant? A mutant is someone with
special powers. Some mutants can fly,
others can create ice, shoot energy
beams from their eyes or control
the weather. Some have great mental
powers and can read minds.

Mutants are people who have evolved to a higher level than ordinary humans. Their special powers usually emerge when they are children. Many have trouble controlling their powers. Some are scared by their amazing abilities.

One man decided to help the mutants and bring them together as the X-Men.

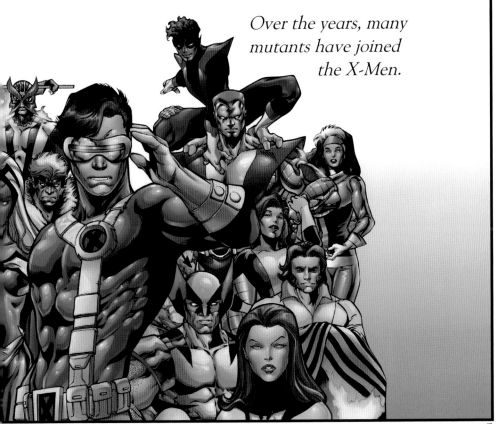

Over the years, many mutants have joined the X-Men.

Professor X

Professor Charles Xavier is the man
who brought the X-Men together.
His students know him as
Professor X. He is also a mutant and
has great mental powers.

He can read the minds of other people. He can also send messages into people's minds. Professor X can make people believe they are seeing or hearing things that aren't really there. His mental powers can be used to stop people from moving or to take away their memories.

Professor X can no longer walk because an alien called Lucifer dropped a massive stone block on him in a fight.

The school

Most mutants just want to get along with humans and be accepted for who they are. But many humans treat them badly. They are afraid of mutants, believing that they are a threat to humans.

Humans are also afraid of mutants because they are different. Some humans want mutants to live apart from them.

Professor X believes that humans and mutants should live together in peace. He hopes that humans can learn not to fear mutants but to treat them as friends with special gifts.

Because of this belief, Professor X started his School for Gifted Youngsters.

The X-Men member Angel rescues a mutant girl from an angry crowd.

Professor X feels it is important for young mutants to have a place where they can learn to use their powers alongside others like themselves. At his School for Gifted Youngsters, they can study in safety, away from human prejudice and hatred.

There, frightened young mutants who are just discovering their powers find comfort and friendship among others like them.

They also find a great teacher in Professor X. The professor trains his students to control their powers and to use them only for good.

The students at the school have many different powers.

The mansion

Professor X owns a large private estate in Westchester County, north of New York City, USA, that includes a great mansion. The professor uses this house and land as the home for his school.

Security is very important at
the school. Professor X installed a steel
front gate protected by an invisible
force field. The beautiful grounds of
the estate contain a swimming pool,
stables, lakes, a boathouse and a maze.

There is a secret, underground hangar hidden from view on the estate. The X-Men's jet, the Blackbird, is kept there. When the Blackbird is needed, it races along an underground runway, then takes off into the sky. A tractor beam guides the Blackbird safely back to the runway and also drives away unwanted visitors.

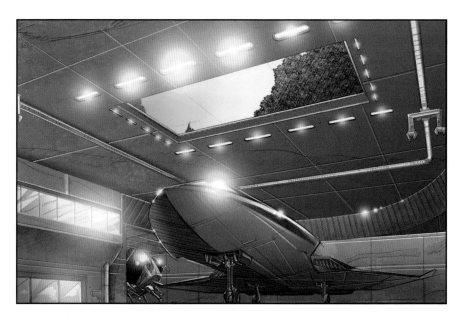

The Blackbird can also take off vertically through an opening in the underground hangar.

The Blackbird can even fly into space.

The mansion itself has dormitories, classrooms and a large kitchen. Professor X often teaches classes in the library. Special high-speed tubes carry students to the mansion's lower levels.

Monorail
An underground monorail zips the X-Men from the mansion to the secret Blackbird hangar in just 20 seconds!

The Danger Room

The most important part of Professor X's training programme takes place in the Danger Room. This is a special training area where the X-Men work hard to improve their athletic and fighting skills. It is the place where mutants practise using their powers during combat.

The Danger Room

Professor X controls special combat robots as they test the fighting skills of the X-Men in the Danger Room.

The Danger Room contains special equipment that challenges the X-Men. Professor X sits in the control room next to the Danger Room. From there, he can train his X-Men to deal with all kinds of danger. Missiles, lasers and alien weapons attack the X-Men. They must react swiftly to these deadly assaults.

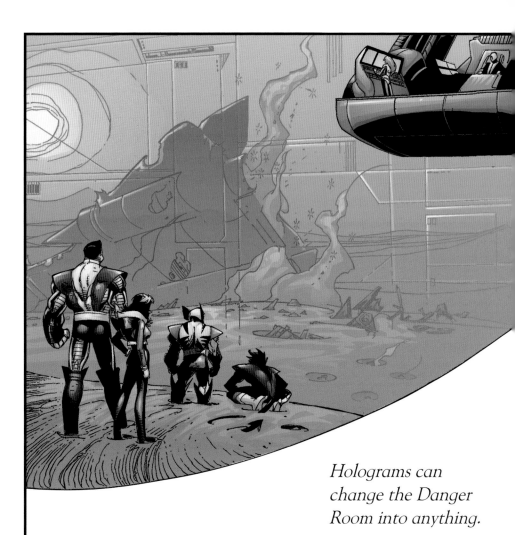

Holograms can change the Danger Room into anything.

Professor X sets traps to surprise his students. Steel nets, giant hammers and a large vice with sharp metal teeth must be avoided. Metal tentacles and jets of flame sometimes lash out at the X-Men training in the Danger Room.

Over the years, the Danger Room has been updated many times. The latest alien technology allows Professor X to create holograms for his X-Men to battle. The holograms can look like any place on Earth or even another planet. They can also look like the X-Men's greatest enemies. Fighting these enemies in the Danger Rooms prepares the X-Men for fighting them in real life.

The first Danger Room was more like a gymnasium with an obstacle course and traps.

Battles fought in the Danger Room feel very real to the X-Men at the school. Professor X believes that this is the only way for his young students to learn to control their powers and find out what combat is like.

Mind machine
Cerebro is Professor X's super computer. When he is connected by a headset, it helps him to locate other mutants.

Right next to the Danger Room is the War Room. The War Room is filled with powerful computers, which collect information from around the world. Large screens in the War Room allow Professor X to keep an eye on his X-Men during actual combat situations.

The War Room

The first students

Scott Summers, also known as Cyclops, was the first student at Professor X's School for Gifted Youngsters. He quickly became Professor X's most trusted ally. Cyclops shares the professor's belief that humans and mutants should live together in peace. Cyclops most often leads the X-Men into battle.

Cyclops absorbs his power from the sun. He uses it to fire ruby-red rays from his eyes.

Special visor
Cyclops's visor blocks
his eye beams. He presses
a button on either side
of the visor to release
his optic blasts.

Cyclops's mutant power is the ability
to shoot powerful beams from his eyes.
These beams are so strong they can
destroy an entire building. Cyclops must
wear special glasses or a visor to stop
the deadly beams.

The beams from Cyclops's eyes can destroy a tank!

*Iceman was
the youngest
of the first
students.*

The second
mutant to arrive
at the school and join
the X-Men was Bobby Drake, known as
Iceman. Iceman can freeze anything,
including his own body. He can shape
moisture from the air into an ice slide
that lets him travel really fast.

The young Bobby Drake only used his freezing power as a last resort when his girlfriend was attacked.

Iceman discovered his powers in his early teens but kept them secret. One night, he used his icy skills to protect his girlfriend from an attacker. A frightened crowd then began attacking Bobby. He was rescued by Professor X and Cyclops, who invited him to become a student at the school.

When Warren
Worthington III was
a teenager, something strange
happened. He grew a pair of wings
from his back. Discovering he was
a mutant, Warren practised in secret,
learning how to fly using his wings.

Wings of an angel
Using his powerful wings, Angel can soar to a height of 3,000 metres (10,000 feet). His wings can fold up under his clothes.

He went to New York City and became a costumed crime fighter. Warren called himself the Avenging Angel.

During this time, Professor X learnt of Warren's ability. He asked Warren to come to the school and join the X-Men. Warren agreed and became known as Angel and later as Archangel.

Like all the X-Men, Angel is a fierce fighter!

Hank McCoy's mutant powers allow him to run fast for long distances and swing from a tree like an acrobat. He is as strong as ten men and is also a brilliant scientist, with a mind almost as amazing as that of Professor X.

The professor invited Hank to join the original X-Men. He was called Beast because of his huge hands and feet.

The formula changed Hank into a giant blue beast!

After he graduated from the school, Beast created a formula to help bring out hidden powers in mutants. When he drank the formula himself, he grew blue fur all over his body.

The last of the original X-Men to come to the school was actually Professor X's first student. As a child, Jean Grey could read minds and place thoughts into other people's heads. She could also move objects with her mind.

Name change
Jean Grey used the name Marvel Girl when she arrived at the school. Later, she was called Phoenix.

As Phoenix, Jean Grey has incredible power.

When she was eleven, Jean was
injured by her own mental abilities.
Her parents sent her to Professor X for
help. He healed her and helped train her
to use her powers. Later, Jean became
a key member of the X-Men and
a teacher at the school.

Famous graduates

Over the years, many mutants have come to study at the School for Gifted Youngsters. A number of them went on to become important members of the X-Men team.

Probably the most famous of all the X-Men is Wolverine. His real name is Logan, and he was born in Canada. As part of a secret government experiment, Wolverine was given a metal skeleton and long, sharp metal claws. Wolverine's mutant power is the ability to heal very quickly from any injury. His healing power, metal skeleton and razor-sharp claws come in handy when he fights.

Wolverine got his name because he is a fierce fighter and can track down his enemies by smell like a wolf.

Another important member of the X-Men team is Ororo Munroe, also known as Storm. She has the power to control the weather. This mutant can create rain, snow, hail, wind, fog or lightning. Storm's powers are connected to the way she feels. When she gets angry, dark clouds gather. If she is very upset, strong winds blow and thunder booms in the sky. At the School for Gifted Youngsters, Professor X taught her how to control her incredible ability. She teaches younger mutants at the school.

Storm was born in Africa.

Rogue's mutant power is both a gift and a curse. She can absorb a person's memories and life energy just by touching them. But that touch can leave the person in a coma.

Rogue came to the school to get help from Professor X to control her absorbing power. She still cannot fully control it. So Rogue must cover her entire body at all times. She always wears gloves to be sure she doesn't accidentally touch and harm anyone.

Rogue can also absorb the powers of other mutants and Super Heroes, although the powers only last short time.

Rogue has incredible strength.

37

Nightcrawler has the power to teleport from one place to another in a split second. Now, he's there, and then – poof! – he vanishes in a puff of smoke, only to reappear in another spot!

Nightcrawler, whose real name is
Kurt Wagner, was born in Germany.
There, he was feared by the villagers
in his small town. They were frightened
by his teleporting power and by
the way he looked.

Professor X
invited him to come
to the school and
join the X-Men.
Like many
other mutants,
Nightcrawler
found a safe home
within the walls of
the X-Men mansion.

*Professor X saved Nightcrawler from the angry villagers
who were trying to kill him.*

Magneto

Professor X started his School for Gifted Youngsters to give mutants a safe home and help train them to use their powers. But he also began the school for another reason – to stop the mutant Magneto.

Magneto does not believe that humans and mutants should live together in peace. He believes that mutants should destroy humans and take over the Earth. Magneto is the greatest threat to Professor X's dream of mutants and humans getting along together.

Professor X and Magneto are deadly enemies.

Magneto is known as the Master of Magnetism. His mutant power is the ability to control metal objects using his magnetic force.

Magneto and Professor X started out as friends. Soon, Magneto's belief that humans should be controlled by mutants made them enemies. Professor X hopes that one day his old friend will see things his way, but for now the battle between the X-Men and Magneto continues.

Mind protector
Magneto's helmet protects him from telepathic attacks. It prevents mutants like Professor X or Jean Grey from reading his mind or controlling his actions.

Generation X

Professor X's School for Gifted Youngsters has been a huge success. For many years, mutants from all over the world have come to the school. They have found a home and a place to develop their special talents.

In time, Professor X got too busy leading the X-Men to also run the school for younger mutants. He moved the school to Massachusetts and gave the running of the school to two experienced X-Men – Sean Cassidy, known as Banshee, and Emma Frost, known as the White Queen. Together, they teach the young mutants known as Generation X.

The mutants of Generation X come from all over the world and have many different powers.

At the new school, the students of Generation X are taught to control their powers and use them for good.

Professor X's dedication to teaching didn't stop when the school moved. He turned his mansion into the Xavier Institute for Higher Learning. There, more experienced mutants could study and improve their skills.

Through both X-Men schools, Professor X hopes his dream of humans and mutants living together in peace will someday come true.

X enemy
The White Queen used to be the X-Men's enemy. In time, she accepted the idea of humans and mutants working together.

Some of the teenage mutants who make up Generation X. They use their mutant powers to help fight the enemies of the X-Men.

Synch

M

Chamber

Jubilee

Husk

Skin

Glossary

acrobat
A circus performer who swings from ropes and trapezes.

alien
A creature who is not human and comes from outer space.

ally
A friend or helper.

assaults
Violent attacks on a person or persons.

challenges
Tests someones skills.

coma
A state of unconsciousness, a bit like sleeping. It is caused by illness or injury.

combat
A fight.

curse
A cause of bad luck.

dedication
Commitment or determination to do something.

dormitories
Large rooms where students sleep.

emerge
Appear.

estate
A large piece of land, usually with a house and many buildings on it.

evolved
Changed very slowly. Humans evolved from apes.

graduates
Students who have finished studying at a school or college.

hangar
A building where aircraft are kept.

holograms
Three-dimensional images made from light that look real.

magnetic force
A power that makes some metals attract each other.

memories
Thoughts of the past.

mental
To do with the mind.

moisture
Water in the form of tiny droplets.

optic
To do with the eyes.

original
The first.

prejudice
Hating people because they are different from you.

security
Protection against danger.

teleport
Move instantly from one place to another.

tentacles
Long arms that bend easily.

vice
A metal tool like a clamp used to hold on to something tightly.

visor
A screen in front of the eyes.